THE BEER REVIEW

★ LOGBOOK

RATE AND RECORD
YOUR FAVORITE BREWS

PETER PAUPER PRESS, INC.
White Plains, New York

Dates this log was kept:

_____ to _____

PETER PAUPER PRESS
Fine Books and Gifts Since 1928

Our Company

In 1928, at the age of twenty-two, Peter Beilenson began printing books on a small press in the basement of his parents' home in Larchmont, New York. Peter—and later, his wife, Edna—sought to create fine books that sold at "prices even a pauper could afford."

Today, still family owned and operated, Peter Pauper Press continues to honor our founders' legacy—and our customers' expectations— of beauty, quality, and value.

Images copyright Mariya II, used under license from Shutterstock.com

With special thanks to Ruth Cullen, much of whose content in *The Little Black Book of Beer* was adapted for this logbook

Compiled by Steve Debara

Designed by David Cole Wheeler

Visit us at www.peterpauper.com

CONTENTS

INTRODUCTION

Beer is perhaps the most indispensable substance ever known to man. So much more than a fermented malt beverage, beer has served as food, drink, medicine, and currency. We always feel just a little smarter, wittier, and more attractive when beer's around. Today we have real choices when selecting beer. The craft brewing renaissance has flooded the market with quality traditional beers and unique specialty brews.

With access to thousands of unique brews, how does one remember all the different components, and recall which beers were worthy and which should be avoided? That's where the *Beer Review Logbook* comes in! Within these log pages, you can record the details—including the date and place, beer name and style, brewer and price, ABV (alcohol by volume), and beer container—that will help you recall each brew. Then rate each beer according to the criteria in categories used by beer judges and aficionados: appearance, aroma, taste, and mouth-feel; and jot down your overall impressions and rating.

The primer on the following pages is a crash course on how to taste and evaluate beers. The descriptions and chart of beer styles provides a big-picture context and frame of reference of the many beer styles and their sub-styles. Keep this little book handy to create a unique travelogue, with your observations and notes in the log pages, of your journey through the world of beer.

Savor the experience!

TASTING AND EVALUATING A BREW

Beer is versatile and dependable, and you can always count on it to liven up the party or wind things down at the end of the day. But make no mistake: Beer is not simple. In terms of depth, complexity, and overall satisfaction, beer rivals—and often surpasses—wine.

Taste buds don't lie. You either like something or you don't. And tasting beer—truly savoring it and appreciating its finer qualities—requires just a few simple observations: appearance, aroma, taste, and mouthfeel.

Appearance

When evaluating a beer's appearance, consider the color, the head of foam, and the clarity.

A beer's color gives you clues about its style, and the best way to accurately view color is through a clear glass. Any glass will do, but a medium-weight, tall glass with a wide mouth works well for most styles of beer.

Tilt the glass to one side and carefully pour the beer down the inside of the glass. Allow the last inch or so of beer to pour directly into the center of the glass so that it produces a head of foam.

- Look at the **color** of the beer. Is it light and pale or dark as molasses? Do you see straw-colored golds, cherry reds, or nut browns?

- Different beer styles and levels of carbonation produce varying degrees of foam. Does the **head** appear thick and creamy or thin and loosely held together? Are the bubbles fast-rising and quick to dissipate? Or are they the size of a pinhead and long–lasting?

- The **clarity** of a beer may indicate the presence of ale yeasts. Is the beer crystal clear, or does it appear somewhat hazy or cloudy?

Aroma

Aromas include hops, malt, ethers, and other aromatics.

The aromas or "bouquet" of a beer reveals much about its flavors.

Swirl the beer to release its aromatics, then lean into your glass and take a big sniff, breathing in the aroma through the nose and mouth.

- **Hops**: Do you detect the scent of flowers? Pine trees? Citrus? Herbs? Apples?

- **Malt**: Does the beer smell sweet, smoky, nutty, or bready? Do you detect a suggestion of caramel or chocolate?

- **Esters**: Are there fruity or spicy elements? Do you smell apricot, black currant, peach, or strawberry, or spices like cinnamon or nutmeg?

- **Other aromatics** could include banana, clove, cassis, cask wood, butterscotch, licorice, honey, maple syrup, vanilla, ginger, and more.

Taste

Tastes can be categorized into hops, malt, balance, and other flavors or factors.

The range of flavors in a beer contributes to its overall taste or "palate," and the way flavors relate to one another is called "balance." Taste is further influenced by the impression of a beer's texture, or body. Beers can be light-bodied, medium-bodied, or full-bodied.

Inhale gently through your nostrils as you take a sip of your beer, allowing the liquid to roll over all areas of your tongue.

- **Hops**: Do you detect the taste of flowers? Pine trees? Citrus? Herbs? Apples? Do you taste nutty sweetness, sharp bitterness, or sour fruit?

- **Malt**: Does the flavor remind you of fresh baked bread, burnt toast, or black espresso? Do you detect a suggestion of caramel or chocolate?

- **Balance**: Do the flavors work together to create a favorable impression?

- **Other**: Alcohol intensity, fruit, spices, licorice, orange peel, honey, maple syrup, seaweed, rum

Mouthfeel

The impression of a beer on the palate is created by body, carbonation, astringency, finish, and other factors.

Swallow a sip of beer, and note the way it feels as it travels down your esophagus.

- **Body**: Does the weight of the beer feel light and crisp, or thick and heavy?

- **Carbonation**: Is the beer fizzy and lively in the mouth, medium, or soft and flat?

- **Astringency**: Does your mouth feel crisp and refreshed? Or is there a distinctly bitter, malty, or yeasty (bready) aftertaste?

- **Finish**: The lasting impression a beer leaves on your senses after you swallow is known as its "finish." The finish includes the lingering taste a beer leaves in your mouth, as well as the warming sensations it creates as you swallow it.

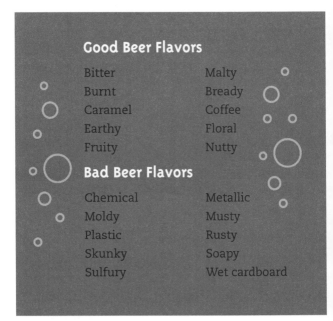

Good Beer Flavors

Bitter	Malty
Burnt	Bready
Caramel	Coffee
Earthy	Floral
Fruity	Nutty

Bad Beer Flavors

Chemical	Metallic
Moldy	Musty
Plastic	Rusty
Skunky	Soapy
Sulfury	Wet cardboard

BASIC BEER STYLES

Learning some basic differences between beer styles provides a frame of reference for your independent beer study as you quench your thirst with new and interesting beers from around the world.

Ales, Lagers, and More

Most beers fall into two main categories: **ales** and **lagers**. Although the terms are used interchangeably to mean "beer," ales and lagers are fundamentally different due to the species of yeast used to make them. All traditional beers were ales fermented by wild yeasts naturally existing in the environment, similar to the types of yeast found in wine and yogurt. These top-fermenting yeasts rise to the surface of liquids during fermentation, which occurs at warmer temperatures in just a matter of days.

Ales are generally fruity, complex, and heavier-tasting beers best served cool (50–60°F). Today, some of the most flavorful beers are made with top-fermenting ale yeasts, but only Belgian lambic-style beers are made the old-fashioned way with naturally occurring wild yeasts.

Lager comes from a German word meaning "to store." Lager beers are made with bottom–fermenting yeasts that ferment at the bottom of liquids at colder temperatures over a period of (usually) four or more weeks. Lagers are typically clear, crisp, and cleaner tasting than ales, and meant to be drunk cold (at 40–50°F). The **pilsner style lager**, famous for its extremely light and clean taste, was first brewed in Pilsen, Bohemia (now the Czech Republic), in 1842. The original Pilsner Urquell brand, though widely imitated, remains the benchmark of this classic style.

Other specialty beers may be distinguished by the manner in which they are brewed or the addition of special flavorings. **Steam beers**, for example, are made with lager yeasts brewed at ale temperatures. **Smoked beers** derive their unique flavor and aroma from malt that has been dried over wood smoke. And the addition of fruit during the fermentation process imparts a wine-like flavor to many **fruit beers**.

Beer Style	Characteristics	Alcohol by Volume (ABV)
ALES		
Barley Wine	Strong, dark, & full-bodied with bitter-sweet, wine-like characteristics	8.4–12.0%
Bitter Ale	Light-bodied & distinctively bitter, ranging in strength & hops intensity from Ordinary to Best to Extra Special (ESB).	3.0–5.8%
Brown Ale	Sweet, malty, & medium-bodied with light hops presence	4.0–6.4%
Mild Ale	Mildly sweet, light-bodied, & low in hops & alcohol	3.2–4.0%
Pale Ale	Dry, hoppy, & medium-bodied with good malt balance	4.0–6.0%
India Pale Ale (IPA)	Strong, dry, & medium-bodied with intense hops aroma & bitterness	5.0–10.5%
Strong Golden Ale	Light-bodied & highly alcoholic with subtle flavors of fruit, spices, & hops	7.0–11.0%
Old Brown & Red Ale	Intensely sour, sweet, & wine-like with complex fruit & malt flavors	4.6–5.2%

Old/ Strong Ale	Strong, dark, & full-bodied with rich fruit & malt flavors	6.0–11.0%
Scottish Ales	Dark, malty, & sweet, ranging in body & strength from light to "wee heavy"	2.8–8.0%
Irish Red Ale	Sweet, medium-bodied, reddish amber ale with caramel malt flavors & medium hop bitterness	4.0–6.0%
Porter	Dark, bitter, & light-bodied with roasted coffee & chocolate flavors	4.5–6.0%
Stout	Very dark, bitter, & medium-bodied with roasted coffee & chocolate flavors	3.0–12.0%
Trappist/ Abbey Ales	Fruity, spicy, & strong with complex flavors & earthy, hoppy aromas	5.0–10.0%
Saison & Bière de Garde	Fruity, spicy, & dry with earthy, floral aromas	4.5–9.0%
Wheat Beer	Crisp & light-bodied with fruit & spice flavors	2.5–5.5%
Lambic	Intensely dry & fruity with complex earthy, cider-like flavors	5.0–7.0%

LAGERS

Bock Beers	Strong, full-bodied, & malty with mild sweetness & mild hopping	6.0–14.4%
Dortmunder /Export Lager	Crisp, golden, & medium-bodied with good malt presence & light hopping	5.0–6.0%
Dark & Black Lagers	Dark & well-balanced with roasted malt flavors, hops bitterness, & a clean, dry finish	3.8–5.0%
Pilsner	Dry, hoppy, & light-bodied with good hops aromas & flavors balanced by malt	4.0–6.0%
Non-Alcoholic Lager	Mildly sweet, light-bodied, & highly carbonated with trace amounts of alcohol	<.5%
Light, Low Carb, Dry, & Ice Lagers	American variations of pilsner style. Mildly sweet, light-bodied, & highly carbonated with low malt & hops presence. Dry lagers have less sweetness, & ice lagers are higher in alcohol.	4.0–6.0%
Pale Lager (Helles)	Medium-bodied & golden with toasted malt flavors & low bitterness	4.5–5.5%

Amber/ Red Lager	Mildly sweet with toasted malt flavors & low hops presence	3.5– 5.9%
Malt Liquor	High in alcohol with very low malt or hops flavors	6.25– 7.5%
	SPECIALTIES & COMBINATION STYLES	
Steam Beer	Clean-tasting & medium-bodied with caramel malt flavors & moderate hops bitterness	4.0– 5.4%
Altbier	Smooth & medium-bodied with crisp hops bitterness & good malt presence	4.3– 5%
Kölsch	Pale, light-bodied, & mildly fruity with low hops bitterness	4.8– 5.3%
Smoked Beer	Full-bodied & malty with smoky aromas & flavors	4.6– 6.3%
Fruit Beer	Crisp & fruity with flavors ranging from very dry to sweet	2.5– 12%
Cream Ale	Light-bodied, mild, & slightly sweet with low hops presence	4.2– 5.6%
Spiced/ Flavored Beers	Varying in intensity & strength, & flavored by assorted spices, vegetables, honey, & other substances	2.5– 12%

★ TASTING NOTES ★

Date _____ Place _____

Beer Name _____

Style _____ ABV _____

Brewer _____ Price _____

Appearance—Color, Head, & Clarity _____
_____

Aroma—Hops, Malt, Ethers, & Other Aromatics _____
_____
_____

Taste—Hops, Malt, Balance, & Other Flavors or Factors _____
_____
_____

Mouthfeel—Body, Carbonation, Astringency, Finish, etc. _____
_____

☐ Draft
☐ Bottle
Overall Impressions _____ ☐ Can

....

RATING

🍺🍺🍺🍺🍺

★ TASTING NOTES ★

Date _____ Place _____

Beer Name _____

Style _____ ABV_____

Brewer _____ Price _____

Appearance—Color, Head, & Clarity _____
_____

Aroma—Hops, Malt, Ethers, & Other Aromatics _____
_____
_____

Taste—Hops, Malt, Balance, & Other Flavors or Factors ____
_____
_____

Mouthfeel—Body, Carbonation, Astringency, Finish, etc. _____
_____

Overall Impressions _____

- ☐ Draft
- ☐ Bottle
- ☐ Can

RATING

☐☐☐☐☐

★ TASTING NOTES ★

Date _____ Place _____

Beer Name _____

Style _____ ABV _____

Brewer _____ Price _____

Appearance—Color, Head, & Clarity _____

Aroma—Hops, Malt, Ethers, & Other Aromatics _____

Taste—Hops, Malt, Balance, & Other Flavors or Factors _____

Mouthfeel—Body, Carbonation, Astringency, Finish, etc. _____

Overall Impressions _____

- [ ] Draft
- [ ] Bottle
- [ ] Can

RATING

☐☐☐☐☐

★ TASTING NOTES ★

Date _____ Place _____

Beer Name _____

Style _____ ABV _____

Brewer _____ Price _____

Appearance—Color, Head, & Clarity _____
_____

Aroma—Hops, Malt, Ethers, & Other Aromatics _____
_____
_____

Taste—Hops, Malt, Balance, & Other Flavors or Factors _____
_____
_____

Mouthfeel—Body, Carbonation, Astringency, Finish, etc. _____
_____
_____

Overall Impressions _____

☐ Draft
☐ Bottle
☐ Can

- - - - - - - - - - -

RATING

⛾ ⛾ ⛾ ⛾ ⛾

★ TASTING NOTES ★

Date _____ Place _____

Beer Name _____

Style _____ ABV_____

Brewer _____ Price _____

Appearance—Color, Head, & Clarity _____
_____

Aroma—Hops, Malt, Ethers, & Other Aromatics _____
_____
_____

Taste—Hops, Malt, Balance, & Other Flavors or Factors _____
_____
_____

Mouthfeel—Body, Carbonation, Astringency, Finish, etc. _____
_____

Overall Impressions _____
_____
_____
_____
_____
_____

☐ Draft
☐ Bottle
☐ Can

. . . .

RATING

⛾ ⛾ ⛾ ⛾ ⛾

★ TASTING NOTES ★

Date _____ Place _____

Beer Name _____

Style _____ ABV _____

Brewer _____ Price _____

Appearance—Color, Head, & Clarity _____
_____

Aroma—Hops, Malt, Ethers, & Other Aromatics _____
_____
_____

Taste—Hops, Malt, Balance, & Other Flavors or Factors _____
_____
_____

Mouthfeel—Body, Carbonation, Astringency, Finish, etc. _____
_____

Overall Impressions _____

☐ Draft
☐ Bottle
☐ Can

RATING

🍺 🍺 🍺 🍺 🍺

★ TASTING NOTES ★

Date _____ Place _____

Beer Name _____

Style _____ ABV_____

Brewer _____ Price _____

Appearance—Color, Head, & Clarity _____
_____

Aroma—Hops, Malt, Ethers, & Other Aromatics _____
_____
_____

Taste—Hops, Malt, Balance, & Other Flavors or Factors _____
_____
_____

Mouthfeel—Body, Carbonation, Astringency, Finish, etc. _____
_____

_____

Overall Impressions _____

☐ Draft

☐ Bottle

☐ Can

RATING

⬜⬜⬜⬜⬜

★ TASTING NOTES ★

Date _____ Place _____

Beer Name _____

Style _____ ABV _____

Brewer _____ Price _____

Appearance—Color, Head, & Clarity _____

_____

Aroma—Hops, Malt, Ethers, & Other Aromatics _____

_____

_____

Taste—Hops, Malt, Balance, & Other Flavors or Factors _____

_____

_____

Mouthfeel—Body, Carbonation, Astringency, Finish, etc. _____

_____

☐ Draft

☐ Bottle

Overall Impressions _____ ☐ Can

RATING

★ TASTING NOTES ★

Date _____ Place _____

Beer Name _____

Style _____ ABV_____

Brewer _____ Price _____

Appearance—Color, Head, & Clarity _____
_____

Aroma—Hops, Malt, Ethers, & Other Aromatics _____
_____
_____

Taste—Hops, Malt, Balance, & Other Flavors or Factors _____
_____
_____

Mouthfeel—Body, Carbonation, Astringency, Finish, etc. _____
_____
_____

Overall Impressions _____

- ☐ Draft
- ☐ Bottle
- ☐ Can

RATING

🍺🍺🍺🍺🍺

★ TASTING NOTES ★

Date _____ Place _____

Beer Name _____

Style _____ ABV _____

Brewer _____ Price _____

Appearance—Color, Head, & Clarity _____
_____

Aroma—Hops, Malt, Ethers, & Other Aromatics _____
_____
_____

Taste—Hops, Malt, Balance, & Other Flavors or Factors _____
_____
_____

Mouthfeel—Body, Carbonation, Astringency, Finish, etc. _____
_____

□ Draft

_____
□ Bottle

Overall Impressions _____
□ Can

· · · · · · · · · · · · · ·

RATING

★ TASTING NOTES ★

Date _____ Place _____

Beer Name _____

Style _____ ABV_____

Brewer _____ Price _____

Appearance—Color, Head, & Clarity _____
_____

Aroma—Hops, Malt, Ethers, & Other Aromatics _____
_____
_____

Taste—Hops, Malt, Balance, & Other Flavors or Factors _____
_____
_____

Mouthfeel—Body, Carbonation, Astringency, Finish, etc. _____
_____

☐ Draft

☐ Bottle

Overall Impressions _____

☐ Can

· · · · · · · · · · ·

RATING

⊔ ⊔ ⊔ ⊔ ⊔

★ TASTING NOTES ★

Date _____ Place _____

Beer Name _____

Style _____ ABV ____

Brewer _____ Price _____

Appearance—Color, Head, & Clarity _____
_____

Aroma—Hops, Malt, Ethers, & Other Aromatics _____
_____
_____

Taste—Hops, Malt, Balance, & Other Flavors or Factors _____
_____
_____

Mouthfeel—Body, Carbonation, Astringency, Finish, etc. _____
_____

_____

Overall Impressions _____

_____

_____

_____

_____

- [ ] Draft
- [ ] Bottle
- [ ] Can

· · · · · · · · · · · ·

RATING

⊔ ⊔ ⊔ ⊔ ⊔

★ TASTING NOTES ★

Date _____ Place _____

Beer Name _____

Style _____ ABV_____

Brewer _____ Price _____

Appearance—Color, Head, & Clarity _____
_____

Aroma—Hops, Malt, Ethers, & Other Aromatics _____
_____
_____

Taste—Hops, Malt, Balance, & Other Flavors or Factors _____
_____
_____

Mouthfeel—Body, Carbonation, Astringency, Finish, etc. _____
_____

Overall Impressions _____

☐ Draft
☐ Bottle
☐ Can

RATING

⛉ ⛉ ⛉ ⛉ ⛉

★ TASTING NOTES ★

Date _____ Place _____

Beer Name _____

Style _____ ABV _____

Brewer _____ Price _____

Appearance—Color, Head, & Clarity _____

_____

Aroma—Hops, Malt, Ethers, & Other Aromatics _____

_____

_____

Taste—Hops, Malt, Balance, & Other Flavors or Factors _____

_____

_____

Mouthfeel—Body, Carbonation, Astringency, Finish, etc. _____

_____

_____

Overall Impressions _____

☐ Draft

☐ Bottle

☐ Can

· · · · · · · · · · · ·

RATING

☐ ☐ ☐ ☐ ☐

★ TASTING NOTES ★

Date _____ Place _____

Beer Name _____

Style _____ ABV _____

Brewer _____ Price _____

Appearance—Color, Head, & Clarity _____
_____

Aroma—Hops, Malt, Ethers, & Other Aromatics _____
_____
_____

Taste—Hops, Malt, Balance, & Other Flavors or Factors _____
_____
_____

Mouthfeel—Body, Carbonation, Astringency, Finish, etc. _____
_____

Overall Impressions _____

☐ Draft
☐ Bottle
☐ Can
. . . .
RATING

ᗡ ᗡ ᗡ ᗡ ᗡ

★ TASTING NOTES ★

Date _____ Place _____

Beer Name _____

Style _____ ABV _____

Brewer _____ Price _____

Appearance—Color, Head, & Clarity _____
_____
_____

Aroma—Hops, Malt, Ethers, & Other Aromatics _____
_____
_____
_____

Taste—Hops, Malt, Balance, & Other Flavors or Factors _____
_____
_____
_____

Mouthfeel—Body, Carbonation, Astringency, Finish, etc. _____
_____
_____

Overall Impressions _____

☐ Draft
☐ Bottle
☐ Can

RATING

🍺🍺🍺🍺🍺

★ TASTING NOTES ★

Date _____ Place _____

Beer Name _____

Style _____ ABV_____

Brewer _____ Price _____

Appearance—Color, Head, & Clarity _____

_____

Aroma—Hops, Malt, Ethers, & Other Aromatics _____

_____

_____

Taste—Hops, Malt, Balance, & Other Flavors or Factors _____

_____

_____

Mouthfeel—Body, Carbonation, Astringency, Finish, etc. _____

_____

_____

Overall Impressions _____

_____

_____

_____

_____

- [ ] Draft
- [ ] Bottle
- [ ] Can

RATING

🍺🍺🍺🍺🍺

★ TASTING NOTES ★

Date _____ Place _____

Beer Name _____

Style _____ ABV_____

Brewer _____ Price _____

Appearance—Color, Head, & Clarity _____
_____

Aroma—Hops, Malt, Ethers, & Other Aromatics _____
_____
_____

Taste—Hops, Malt, Balance, & Other Flavors or Factors _____
_____
_____

Mouthfeel—Body, Carbonation, Astringency, Finish, etc. _____
_____

Overall Impressions _____

☐ Draft
☐ Bottle
☐ Can

· · · · · · · · · · · · · ·

RATING

⬜⬜⬜⬜⬜

★ TASTING NOTES ★

Date _____ Place _____

Beer Name _____

Style _____ ABV _____

Brewer _____ Price _____

Appearance—Color, Head, & Clarity _____
_____

Aroma—Hops, Malt, Ethers, & Other Aromatics _____
_____
_____

Taste—Hops, Malt, Balance, & Other Flavors or Factors _____
_____
_____

Mouthfeel—Body, Carbonation, Astringency, Finish, etc. _____
_____

Overall Impressions _____

☐ Draft
☐ Bottle
☐ Can

....

RATING

⊔ ⊔ ⊔ ⊔ ⊔

★ TASTING NOTES ★

Date _____ Place _____

Beer Name _____

Style _____ ABV____

Brewer _____ Price _____

Appearance—Color, Head, & Clarity _____
_____

Aroma—Hops, Malt, Ethers, & Other Aromatics _____
_____
_____

Taste—Hops, Malt, Balance, & Other Flavors or Factors _____
_____
_____

Mouthfeel—Body, Carbonation, Astringency, Finish, etc. _____
_____

_____

Overall Impressions _____
_____
_____
_____
_____

☐ Draft
☐ Bottle
☐ Can

· · · · · · · · · · · · ·

RATING

🍺🍺🍺🍺🍺

★ TASTING NOTES ★

Date _____ Place _____

Beer Name _____

Style _____ ABV _____

Brewer _____ Price _____

Appearance—Color, Head, & Clarity _____
_____

Aroma—Hops, Malt, Ethers, & Other Aromatics _____
_____
_____

Taste—Hops, Malt, Balance, & Other Flavors or Factors _____
_____
_____

Mouthfeel—Body, Carbonation, Astringency, Finish, etc. _____
_____

Overall Impressions _____

☐ Draft
☐ Bottle
☐ Can

. . . .

RATING

▢ ▢ ▢ ▢ ▢

★ TASTING NOTES ★

Date _____ Place _____

Beer Name _____

Style _____ ABV _____

Brewer _____ Price _____

Appearance—Color, Head, & Clarity _____
_____

Aroma—Hops, Malt, Ethers, & Other Aromatics _____
_____
_____

Taste—Hops, Malt, Balance, & Other Flavors or Factors _____
_____
_____

Mouthfeel—Body, Carbonation, Astringency, Finish, etc. _____
_____

□ Draft

Overall Impressions _____

□ Bottle

□ Can

· · · · · · · · · · · · ·

RATING

🍺 🍺 🍺 🍺 🍺

★ TASTING NOTES ★

Date _____ Place _____

Beer Name _____

Style _____ ABV _____

Brewer _____ Price _____

Appearance—Color, Head, & Clarity _____
_____

Aroma—Hops, Malt, Ethers, & Other Aromatics _____
_____
_____

Taste—Hops, Malt, Balance, & Other Flavors or Factors _____
_____
_____

Mouthfeel—Body, Carbonation, Astringency, Finish, etc. _____
_____

_____

Overall Impressions _____

_____

_____

_____

_____

☐ Draft
☐ Bottle
☐ Can

. . . .

RATING

🍺 🍺 🍺 🍺 🍺

★ TASTING NOTES ★

Date _____ Place _____

Beer Name _____

Style _____ ABV _____

Brewer _____ Price _____

Appearance—Color, Head, & Clarity _____
_____

Aroma—Hops, Malt, Ethers, & Other Aromatics _____
_____
_____

Taste—Hops, Malt, Balance, & Other Flavors or Factors _____
_____
_____

Mouthfeel—Body, Carbonation, Astringency, Finish, etc. _____
_____
_____

Overall Impressions _____

☐ Draft
☐ Bottle
☐ Can

. . . .

RATING

🍺 🍺 🍺 🍺 🍺

★ TASTING NOTES ★

Date _____ Place _____

Beer Name _____

Style _____ ABV_____

Brewer _____ Price _____

Appearance—Color, Head, & Clarity _____
_____

Aroma—Hops, Malt, Ethers, & Other Aromatics _____
_____
_____

Taste—Hops, Malt, Balance, & Other Flavors or Factors _____
_____
_____

Mouthfeel—Body, Carbonation, Astringency, Finish, etc. _____
_____

Overall Impressions _____

☐ Draft
☐ Bottle
☐ Can

....

RATING

🍺 🍺 🍺 🍺 🍺

★ TASTING NOTES ★

Date _____ Place _____

Beer Name _____

Style _____ ABV _____

Brewer _____ Price _____

Appearance—Color, Head, & Clarity _____
_____

Aroma—Hops, Malt, Ethers, & Other Aromatics _____
_____
_____

Taste—Hops, Malt, Balance, & Other Flavors or Factors _____
_____
_____

Mouthfeel—Body, Carbonation, Astringency, Finish, etc. _____
_____

Overall Impressions _____

☐ Draft
☐ Bottle
☐ Can

· · · · · · · · · · · ·

RATING

🍺 🍺 🍺 🍺 🍺

★ TASTING NOTES ★

Date _____ Place _____

Beer Name _____

Style _____ ABV _____

Brewer _____ Price _____

Appearance—Color, Head, & Clarity _____
_____

Aroma—Hops, Malt, Ethers, & Other Aromatics _____
_____
_____

Taste—Hops, Malt, Balance, & Other Flavors or Factors _____
_____
_____

Mouthfeel—Body, Carbonation, Astringency, Finish, etc. _____
_____

Overall Impressions _____
_____
_____
_____
_____

☐ Draft
☐ Bottle
☐ Can

RATING

🍺🍺🍺🍺🍺

★ TASTING NOTES ★

Date _____ Place _____

Beer Name _____

Style _____ ABV _____

Brewer _____ Price _____

Appearance—Color, Head, & Clarity _____
_____

Aroma—Hops, Malt, Ethers, & Other Aromatics _____
_____
_____

Taste—Hops, Malt, Balance, & Other Flavors or Factors _____
_____
_____

Mouthfeel—Body, Carbonation, Astringency, Finish, etc. _____
_____

☐ Draft
☐ Bottle
Overall Impressions _____
☐ Can
. . . .
RATING
🍺🍺🍺🍺🍺

★ TASTING NOTES ★

Date _____ Place _____

Beer Name _____

Style _____ ABV_____

Brewer _____ Price _____

Appearance—Color, Head, & Clarity _____
_____

Aroma—Hops, Malt, Ethers, & Other Aromatics _____
_____
_____

Taste—Hops, Malt, Balance, & Other Flavors or Factors _____
_____
_____

Mouthfeel—Body, Carbonation, Astringency, Finish, etc. _____
_____
_____

Overall Impressions _____

- [ ] Draft
- [ ] Bottle
- [ ] Can

. . . .

RATING

⊔ ⊔ ⊔ ⊔ ⊔

★ TASTING NOTES ★

Date _____ Place _____

Beer Name _____

Style _____ ABV_____

Brewer _____ Price _____

Appearance—Color, Head, & Clarity _____
_____

Aroma—Hops, Malt, Ethers, & Other Aromatics _____
_____
_____

Taste—Hops, Malt, Balance, & Other Flavors or Factors _____
_____
_____

Mouthfeel—Body, Carbonation, Astringency, Finish, etc. _____
_____

_____   ☐ Draft

Overall Impressions _____   ☐ Bottle

_____   ☐ Can

_____   · · · · · · · · · · · ·

_____   RATING

_____   ⎕ ⎕ ⎕ ⎕ ⎕

_____

★ TASTING NOTES ★

Date _____ Place _____

Beer Name _____

Style _____ ABV _____

Brewer _____ Price _____

Appearance—Color, Head, & Clarity _____
_____

Aroma—Hops, Malt, Ethers, & Other Aromatics _____
_____
_____

Taste—Hops, Malt, Balance, & Other Flavors or Factors _____
_____
_____

Mouthfeel—Body, Carbonation, Astringency, Finish, etc. _____
_____

Overall Impressions _____

☐ Draft
☐ Bottle
☐ Can

....

RATING

⛉ ⛉ ⛉ ⛉ ⛉

★ TASTING NOTES ★

Date _____ Place _____

Beer Name _____

Style _____ ABV _____

Brewer _____ Price _____

Appearance—Color, Head, & Clarity _____
_____

Aroma—Hops, Malt, Ethers, & Other Aromatics _____
_____
_____

Taste—Hops, Malt, Balance, & Other Flavors or Factors _____
_____
_____

Mouthfeel—Body, Carbonation, Astringency, Finish, etc. _____
_____

Overall Impressions _____

- ☐ Draft
- ☐ Bottle
- ☐ Can

. . . .
RATING

🍺 🍺 🍺 🍺 🍺

★ TASTING NOTES ★

Date _____ Place _____

Beer Name _____

Style _____ ABV_____

Brewer _____ Price _____

Appearance—Color, Head, & Clarity _____
_____

Aroma—Hops, Malt, Ethers, & Other Aromatics _____
_____
_____

Taste—Hops, Malt, Balance, & Other Flavors or Factors _____
_____
_____

Mouthfeel—Body, Carbonation, Astringency, Finish, etc. _____
_____

Overall Impressions _____

☐ Draft
☐ Bottle
☐ Can
. . . .
RATING
🍺🍺🍺🍺🍺

★ TASTING NOTES ★

Date _____ Place _____

Beer Name _____

Style _____ ABV _____

Brewer _____ Price _____

Appearance—Color, Head, & Clarity _____
_____

Aroma—Hops, Malt, Ethers, & Other Aromatics _____
_____
_____

Taste—Hops, Malt, Balance, & Other Flavors or Factors _____
_____
_____

Mouthfeel—Body, Carbonation, Astringency, Finish, etc. _____
_____
_____

Overall Impressions _____

☐ Draft
☐ Bottle
☐ Can

. . . .

RATING

☐☐☐☐☐

★ TASTING NOTES ★

Date _____ Place _____

Beer Name _____

Style _____ ABV _____

Brewer _____ Price _____

Appearance—Color, Head, & Clarity _____

Aroma—Hops, Malt, Ethers, & Other Aromatics _____

Taste—Hops, Malt, Balance, & Other Flavors or Factors _____

Mouthfeel—Body, Carbonation, Astringency, Finish, etc. _____

Overall Impressions _____

- [ ] Draft
- [ ] Bottle
- [ ] Can

· · · · · · · · · · · · ·

RATING

🍺 🍺 🍺 🍺 🍺

★ TASTING NOTES ★

Date _____ Place _____

Beer Name _____

Style _____ ABV _____

Brewer _____ Price _____

Appearance—Color, Head, & Clarity _____
_____

Aroma—Hops, Malt, Ethers, & Other Aromatics _____
_____

Taste—Hops, Malt, Balance, & Other Flavors or Factors _____
_____
_____

Mouthfeel—Body, Carbonation, Astringency, Finish, etc. _____
_____

_____

Overall Impressions _____
_____
_____
_____
_____
_____
_____

☐ Draft
☐ Bottle
☐ Can

....

RATING

🍺 🍺 🍺 🍺 🍺

★ TASTING NOTES ★

Date _____ Place _____

Beer Name _____

Style _____ ABV _____

Brewer _____ Price _____

Appearance—Color, Head, & Clarity _____
_____

Aroma—Hops, Malt, Ethers, & Other Aromatics _____
_____
_____

Taste—Hops, Malt, Balance, & Other Flavors or Factors _____
_____
_____

Mouthfeel—Body, Carbonation, Astringency, Finish, etc. _____
_____

Overall Impressions _____
_____
_____
_____
_____

☐ Draft
☐ Bottle
☐ Can

RATING

★ TASTING NOTES ★

Date _____ Place _____

Beer Name _____

Style _____ ABV _____

Brewer _____ Price _____

Appearance—Color, Head, & Clarity _____
_____

Aroma—Hops, Malt, Ethers, & Other Aromatics _____
_____
_____

Taste—Hops, Malt, Balance, & Other Flavors or Factors _____
_____
_____

Mouthfeel—Body, Carbonation, Astringency, Finish, etc. _____
_____

Overall Impressions _____
_____

☐ Draft
☐ Bottle
☐ Can

. . . .

RATING

🍺 🍺 🍺 🍺 🍺

★ TASTING NOTES ★

Date _____ Place _____

Beer Name _____

Style _____ ABV_____

Brewer _____ Price _____

Appearance—Color, Head, & Clarity _____

_____

Aroma—Hops, Malt, Ethers, & Other Aromatics _____

_____

_____

Taste—Hops, Malt, Balance, & Other Flavors or Factors _____

_____

_____

Mouthfeel—Body, Carbonation, Astringency, Finish, etc. _____

_____

Overall Impressions _____

☐ Draft
☐ Bottle
☐ Can

. . . .

RATING

☐☐☐☐☐

★ TASTING NOTES ★

Date _____ Place _____

Beer Name _____

Style _____ ABV _____

Brewer _____ Price _____

Appearance—Color, Head, & Clarity _____
_____

Aroma—Hops, Malt, Ethers, & Other Aromatics _____
_____
_____

Taste—Hops, Malt, Balance, & Other Flavors or Factors _____
_____
_____

Mouthfeel—Body, Carbonation, Astringency, Finish, etc. _____
_____

Overall Impressions _____

☐ Draft
☐ Bottle
☐ Can

RATING

☐ ☐ ☐ ☐ ☐

★ TASTING NOTES ★

Date _____ Place _____

Beer Name _____

Style _____ ABV _____

Brewer _____ Price _____

Appearance—Color, Head, & Clarity _____
_____

Aroma—Hops, Malt, Ethers, & Other Aromatics _____
_____
_____

Taste—Hops, Malt, Balance, & Other Flavors or Factors _____
_____
_____

Mouthfeel—Body, Carbonation, Astringency, Finish, etc. _____
_____

Overall Impressions _____

☐ Draft
☐ Bottle
☐ Can

RATING

★ TASTING NOTES ★

Date _____ Place _____

Beer Name _____

Style _____ ABV_____

Brewer _____ Price _____

Appearance—Color, Head, & Clarity _____

_____

Aroma—Hops, Malt, Ethers, & Other Aromatics _____

_____

_____

Taste—Hops, Malt, Balance, & Other Flavors or Factors _____

_____

_____

Mouthfeel—Body, Carbonation, Astringency, Finish, etc. _____

_____

_____

Overall Impressions _____

☐ Draft

☐ Bottle

☐ Can

....

RATING

⌷ ⌷ ⌷ ⌷ ⌷

★ TASTING NOTES ★

Date _____ Place _____

Beer Name _____

Style _____ ABV _____

Brewer _____ Price _____

Appearance—Color, Head, & Clarity _____
_____

Aroma—Hops, Malt, Ethers, & Other Aromatics _____
_____
_____

Taste—Hops, Malt, Balance, & Other Flavors or Factors _____
_____
_____

Mouthfeel—Body, Carbonation, Astringency, Finish, etc. _____
_____

Overall Impressions _____
_____
_____
_____
_____

☐ Draft
☐ Bottle
☐ Can

• • • • • • • • • • • • •

RATING

🍺 🍺 🍺 🍺 🍺

★ TASTING NOTES ★

Date _____ Place _____

Beer Name _____

Style _____ ABV _____

Brewer _____ Price _____

Appearance—Color, Head, & Clarity _____

_____

Aroma—Hops, Malt, Ethers, & Other Aromatics _____

_____

_____

Taste—Hops, Malt, Balance, & Other Flavors or Factors _____

_____

_____

Mouthfeel—Body, Carbonation, Astringency, Finish, etc. _____

_____

Overall Impressions _____

_____

_____

_____

_____

☐ Draft
☐ Bottle
☐ Can

....

RATING

🍺🍺🍺🍺🍺

★ TASTING NOTES ★

Date _____ Place _____

Beer Name _____

Style _____ ABV_____

Brewer _____ Price _____

Appearance—Color, Head, & Clarity _____

_____

Aroma—Hops, Malt, Ethers, & Other Aromatics _____

_____

_____

Taste—Hops, Malt, Balance, & Other Flavors or Factors _____

_____

_____

Mouthfeel—Body, Carbonation, Astringency, Finish, etc. _____

_____

Overall Impressions _____

- ☐ Draft
- ☐ Bottle
- ☐ Can

. . . .

RATING

🍺 🍺 🍺 🍺 🍺

★ TASTING NOTES ★

Date _____ Place _____

Beer Name _____

Style _____ ABV _____

Brewer _____ Price _____

Appearance—Color, Head, & Clarity _____
_____

Aroma—Hops, Malt, Ethers, & Other Aromatics _____
_____
_____

Taste—Hops, Malt, Balance, & Other Flavors or Factors _____
_____
_____

Mouthfeel—Body, Carbonation, Astringency, Finish, etc. _____
_____

Overall Impressions _____

☐ Draft
☐ Bottle
☐ Can

• • • • • • • • • • • • •
RATING
🍺 🍺 🍺 🍺 🍺

★ TASTING NOTES ★

Date _____ Place _____

Beer Name _____

Style _____ ABV_____

Brewer _____ Price _____

Appearance—Color, Head, & Clarity _____

_____

Aroma—Hops, Malt, Ethers, & Other Aromatics _____

_____

_____

Taste—Hops, Malt, Balance, & Other Flavors or Factors _____

_____

_____

Mouthfeel—Body, Carbonation, Astringency, Finish, etc. _____

_____

Overall Impressions _____

☐ Draft
☐ Bottle
☐ Can

· · · · · · · · · ·

RATING

🍺 🍺 🍺 🍺 🍺

★ TASTING NOTES ★

Date _____ Place _____

Beer Name _____

Style _____ ABV_____

Brewer _____ Price _____

Appearance—Color, Head, & Clarity _____
_____

Aroma—Hops, Malt, Ethers, & Other Aromatics _____
_____
_____

Taste—Hops, Malt, Balance, & Other Flavors or Factors _____
_____
_____

Mouthfeel—Body, Carbonation, Astringency, Finish, etc. _____
_____

Overall Impressions _____
_____
_____
_____
_____

- ☐ Draft
- ☐ Bottle
- ☐ Can

RATING

☖ ☖ ☖ ☖ ☖

★ TASTING NOTES ★

Date _____ Place _____

Beer Name _____

Style _____ ABV ____

Brewer _____ Price _____

Appearance—Color, Head, & Clarity _____
_____

Aroma—Hops, Malt, Ethers, & Other Aromatics _____
_____
_____

Taste—Hops, Malt, Balance, & Other Flavors or Factors _____
_____
_____

Mouthfeel—Body, Carbonation, Astringency, Finish, etc. _____
_____

Overall Impressions _____

□ Draft
□ Bottle
□ Can
· · · · · · · · · · · ·
RATING

🍺 🍺 🍺 🍺 🍺

★ TASTING NOTES ★

Date _____ Place _____

Beer Name _____

Style _____ ABV _____

Brewer _____ Price _____

Appearance—Color, Head, & Clarity _____
_____

Aroma—Hops, Malt, Ethers, & Other Aromatics _____
_____
_____

Taste—Hops, Malt, Balance, & Other Flavors or Factors _____
_____
_____

Mouthfeel—Body, Carbonation, Astringency, Finish, etc. _____
_____

Overall Impressions _____

☐ Draft
☐ Bottle
☐ Can

RATING

🍺 🍺 🍺 🍺 🍺

★ TASTING NOTES ★

Date _____ Place _____

Beer Name _____

Style _____ ABV _____

Brewer _____ Price _____

Appearance—Color, Head, & Clarity _____
_____

Aroma—Hops, Malt, Ethers, & Other Aromatics _____
_____
_____

Taste—Hops, Malt, Balance, & Other Flavors or Factors _____
_____
_____

Mouthfeel—Body, Carbonation, Astringency, Finish, etc. _____
_____

Overall Impressions _____

☐ Draft
☐ Bottle
☐ Can

. . . .

RATING

🍺 🍺 🍺 🍺 🍺

★ TASTING NOTES ★

Date _____ Place _____

Beer Name _____

Style _____ ABV ____

Brewer _____ Price _____

Appearance—Color, Head, & Clarity _____
_____

Aroma—Hops, Malt, Ethers, & Other Aromatics _____
_____
_____

Taste—Hops, Malt, Balance, & Other Flavors or Factors _____
_____
_____

Mouthfeel—Body, Carbonation, Astringency, Finish, etc. _____
_____

Overall Impressions _____

- ☐ Draft
- ☐ Bottle
- ☐ Can

· · · · · · · · · · · · · ·

RATING

☐☐☐☐☐

★ TASTING NOTES ★

Date _____ Place _____

Beer Name _____

Style _____ ABV ____

Brewer _____ Price _____

Appearance—Color, Head, & Clarity _____
_____

Aroma—Hops, Malt, Ethers, & Other Aromatics _____
_____
_____

Taste—Hops, Malt, Balance, & Other Flavors or Factors ____
_____
_____

Mouthfeel—Body, Carbonation, Astringency, Finish, etc. ____
_____

Overall Impressions _____

☐ Draft
☐ Bottle
☐ Can

· · · · · · · · · ·

RATING

▯ ▯ ▯ ▯ ▯

★ TASTING NOTES ★

Date _____ Place _____

Beer Name _____

Style _____ ABV _____

Brewer _____ Price _____

Appearance—Color, Head, & Clarity _____
_____

Aroma—Hops, Malt, Ethers, & Other Aromatics _____
_____
_____

Taste—Hops, Malt, Balance, & Other Flavors or Factors _____
_____
_____

Mouthfeel—Body, Carbonation, Astringency, Finish, etc. _____
_____
_____

Overall Impressions _____
_____
_____
_____
_____
_____

☐ Draft
☐ Bottle
☐ Can

. . . .

RATING

☐ ☐ ☐ ☐ ☐

★ TASTING NOTES ★

Date _____ Place _____

Beer Name _____

Style _____ ABV _____

Brewer _____ Price _____

Appearance—Color, Head, & Clarity _____
_____

Aroma—Hops, Malt, Ethers, & Other Aromatics _____
_____
_____

Taste—Hops, Malt, Balance, & Other Flavors or Factors _____
_____
_____

Mouthfeel—Body, Carbonation, Astringency, Finish, etc. _____
_____
_____

Overall Impressions _____
_____
_____
_____
_____

☐ Draft
☐ Bottle
☐ Can

· · · · · · · · · · · · ·

RATING

🍺 🍺 🍺 🍺 🍺

★ TASTING NOTES ★

Date _____ Place _____

Beer Name _____

Style _____ ABV_____

Brewer _____ Price _____

Appearance—Color, Head, & Clarity _____
_____

Aroma—Hops, Malt, Ethers, & Other Aromatics _____
_____
_____

Taste—Hops, Malt, Balance, & Other Flavors or Factors _____
_____
_____

Mouthfeel—Body, Carbonation, Astringency, Finish, etc. _____
_____

Overall Impressions _____

☐ Draft
☐ Bottle
☐ Can

· · · · · · · · · · · · ·
RATING

◢◣◢◣◢◣◢◣◢◣

★ TASTING NOTES ★

Date _____ Place _____

Beer Name _____

Style _____ ABV _____

Brewer _____ Price _____

Appearance—Color, Head, & Clarity _____
_____

Aroma—Hops, Malt, Ethers, & Other Aromatics _____
_____
_____

Taste—Hops, Malt, Balance, & Other Flavors or Factors _____
_____
_____

Mouthfeel—Body, Carbonation, Astringency, Finish, etc. _____
_____
_____

Overall Impressions _____

☐ Draft
☐ Bottle
☐ Can

· · · · · · · · · ·

RATING

⊔ ⊔ ⊔ ⊔ ⊔

★ TASTING NOTES ★

Date _____ Place _____

Beer Name _____

Style _____ ABV ____

Brewer _____ Price _____

Appearance—Color, Head, & Clarity _____
_____

Aroma—Hops, Malt, Ethers, & Other Aromatics _____
_____
_____

Taste—Hops, Malt, Balance, & Other Flavors or Factors ____
_____
_____

Mouthfeel—Body, Carbonation, Astringency, Finish, etc. ____
_____

Overall Impressions _____

☐ Draft
☐ Bottle
☐ Can

. . . .

RATING

☐ ☐ ☐ ☐ ☐

★ TASTING NOTES ★

Date _____ Place _____

Beer Name _____

Style _____ ABV _____

Brewer _____ Price _____

Appearance—Color, Head, & Clarity _____
_____

Aroma—Hops, Malt, Ethers, & Other Aromatics _____
_____
_____

Taste—Hops, Malt, Balance, & Other Flavors or Factors _____
_____
_____

Mouthfeel—Body, Carbonation, Astringency, Finish, etc. _____
_____

Overall Impressions _____

☐ Draft
☐ Bottle
☐ Can

RATING

□□□□□

★ TASTING NOTES ★

Date _____ Place _____

Beer Name _____

Style _____ ABV _____

Brewer _____ Price _____

Appearance—Color, Head, & Clarity _____
_____

Aroma—Hops, Malt, Ethers, & Other Aromatics _____
_____
_____

Taste—Hops, Malt, Balance, & Other Flavors or Factors _____
_____
_____

Mouthfeel—Body, Carbonation, Astringency, Finish, etc. _____
_____

Overall Impressions _____

☐ Draft
☐ Bottle
☐ Can

· · · · · · · · · · · · ·

RATING

⑂ ⑂ ⑂ ⑂ ⑂

★ TASTING NOTES ★

Date _____ Place _____

Beer Name _____

Style _____ ABV_____

Brewer _____ Price _____

Appearance—Color, Head, & Clarity _____
_____

Aroma—Hops, Malt, Ethers, & Other Aromatics _____
_____
_____

Taste—Hops, Malt, Balance, & Other Flavors or Factors _____
_____
_____

Mouthfeel—Body, Carbonation, Astringency, Finish, etc. _____
_____

Overall Impressions _____

☐ Draft
☐ Bottle
☐ Can

. . . .

RATING

⊔ ⊔ ⊔ ⊔ ⊔

★ TASTING NOTES ★

Date _____ Place _____

Beer Name _____

Style _____ ABV _____

Brewer _____ Price _____

Appearance—Color, Head, & Clarity _____
_____

Aroma—Hops, Malt, Ethers, & Other Aromatics _____
_____
_____

Taste—Hops, Malt, Balance, & Other Flavors or Factors _____
_____
_____

Mouthfeel—Body, Carbonation, Astringency, Finish, etc. _____
_____

Overall Impressions _____

☐ Draft
☐ Bottle
☐ Can

· · · · · · · · · · · ·

RATING

⬺ ⬺ ⬺ ⬺ ⬺

★ TASTING NOTES ★

Date _____ Place _____

Beer Name _____

Style _____ ABV_____

Brewer _____ Price _____

Appearance—Color, Head, & Clarity _____
_____

Aroma—Hops, Malt, Ethers, & Other Aromatics _____
_____
_____

Taste—Hops, Malt, Balance, & Other Flavors or Factors _____
_____
_____

Mouthfeel—Body, Carbonation, Astringency, Finish, etc. _____
_____
_____

Overall Impressions _____

☐ Draft
☐ Bottle
☐ Can

....

RATING

🍺 🍺 🍺 🍺 🍺

★ TASTING NOTES ★

Date _____ Place _____

Beer Name _____

Style _____ ABV_____

Brewer _____ Price _____

Appearance—Color, Head, & Clarity _____
_____

Aroma—Hops, Malt, Ethers, & Other Aromatics _____
_____
_____

Taste—Hops, Malt, Balance, & Other Flavors or Factors _____
_____
_____

Mouthfeel—Body, Carbonation, Astringency, Finish, etc. _____
_____

Overall Impressions _____

☐ Draft
☐ Bottle
☐ Can

RATING

⬜⬜⬜⬜⬜

★ TASTING NOTES ★

Date _____ Place _____

Beer Name _____

Style _____ ABV_____

Brewer _____ Price _____

Appearance—Color, Head, & Clarity _____

_____

Aroma—Hops, Malt, Ethers, & Other Aromatics _____

_____

_____

Taste—Hops, Malt, Balance, & Other Flavors or Factors _____

_____

_____

Mouthfeel—Body, Carbonation, Astringency, Finish, etc. _____

_____

_____   ☐ Draft

Overall Impressions _____   ☐ Bottle

_____   ☐ Can

_____   . . . .

_____   RATING

_____   ⛾ ⛾ ⛾ ⛾ ⛾

★ TASTING NOTES ★

Date _____ Place _____

Beer Name _____

Style _____ ABV ____

Brewer _____ Price _____

Appearance—Color, Head, & Clarity _____

_____

Aroma—Hops, Malt, Ethers, & Other Aromatics _____

_____

_____

Taste—Hops, Malt, Balance, & Other Flavors or Factors _____

_____

_____

Mouthfeel—Body, Carbonation, Astringency, Finish, etc. _____

_____

Overall Impressions _____

- ☐ Draft
- ☐ Bottle
- ☐ Can

. . . .

RATING

🍺 🍺 🍺 🍺 🍺

★ TASTING NOTES ★

Date _____ Place _____

Beer Name _____

Style _____ ABV____

Brewer _____ Price _____

Appearance—Color, Head, & Clarity _____
_____

Aroma—Hops, Malt, Ethers, & Other Aromatics _____
_____
_____

Taste—Hops, Malt, Balance, & Other Flavors or Factors _____
_____
_____

Mouthfeel—Body, Carbonation, Astringency, Finish, etc. _____
_____

Overall Impressions _____
_____

☐ Draft
☐ Bottle
☐ Can

RATING

⬜⬜⬜⬜⬜

★ TASTING NOTES ★

Date _____ Place _____

Beer Name _____

Style _____ ABV_____

Brewer _____ Price _____

Appearance—Color, Head, & Clarity _____
_____

Aroma—Hops, Malt, Ethers, & Other Aromatics _____
_____
_____

Taste—Hops, Malt, Balance, & Other Flavors or Factors _____
_____
_____

Mouthfeel—Body, Carbonation, Astringency, Finish, etc. _____
_____

Overall Impressions _____
_____
_____
_____
_____
_____

☐ Draft
☐ Bottle
☐ Can

RATING

🍺 🍺 🍺 🍺 🍺

★ TASTING NOTES ★

Date _____ Place _____

Beer Name _____

Style _____ ABV _____

Brewer _____ Price _____

Appearance—Color, Head, & Clarity _____
_____

Aroma—Hops, Malt, Ethers, & Other Aromatics _____
_____
_____

Taste—Hops, Malt, Balance, & Other Flavors or Factors ____
_____
_____

Mouthfeel—Body, Carbonation, Astringency, Finish, etc. ____
_____

_____

Overall Impressions _____

_____

_____

_____

_____

☐ Draft
☐ Bottle
☐ Can

. . . .

RATING

🍺 🍺 🍺 🍺 🍺

★ TASTING NOTES ★

Date _____ Place _____

Beer Name _____

Style _____ ABV_____

Brewer _____ Price _____

Appearance—Color, Head, & Clarity _____
_____

Aroma—Hops, Malt, Ethers, & Other Aromatics _____
_____
_____

Taste—Hops, Malt, Balance, & Other Flavors or Factors _____
_____
_____

Mouthfeel—Body, Carbonation, Astringency, Finish, etc. _____
_____
_____

Overall Impressions _____

☐ Draft
☐ Bottle
☐ Can

RATING

⊔ ⊔ ⊔ ⊔ ⊔

★ TASTING NOTES ★

Date _____ Place _____

Beer Name _____

Style _____ ABV _____

Brewer _____ Price _____

Appearance—Color, Head, & Clarity _____

_____

Aroma—Hops, Malt, Ethers, & Other Aromatics _____

_____

_____

Taste—Hops, Malt, Balance, & Other Flavors or Factors _____

_____

_____

Mouthfeel—Body, Carbonation, Astringency, Finish, etc. _____

_____

☐ Draft

Overall Impressions _____ ☐ Bottle

☐ Can

_____

RATING

_____

_____

_____

★ TASTING NOTES ★

Date _____ Place _____

Beer Name _____

Style _____ ABV _____

Brewer _____ Price _____

Appearance—Color, Head, & Clarity _____
_____

Aroma—Hops, Malt, Ethers, & Other Aromatics _____
_____
_____

Taste—Hops, Malt, Balance, & Other Flavors or Factors _____
_____
_____

Mouthfeel—Body, Carbonation, Astringency, Finish, etc. _____
_____

Overall Impressions _____

☐ Draft
☐ Bottle
☐ Can

· · · · · · · · · · · · ·

RATING

◻◻◻◻◻

★ TASTING NOTES ★

Date _____ Place _____

Beer Name _____

Style _____ ABV ____

Brewer _____ Price ____

Appearance—Color, Head, & Clarity _____

Aroma—Hops, Malt, Ethers, & Other Aromatics _____

Taste—Hops, Malt, Balance, & Other Flavors or Factors _____

Mouthfeel—Body, Carbonation, Astringency, Finish, etc. _____

Overall Impressions _____

☐ Draft
☐ Bottle
☐ Can

RATING

★ TASTING NOTES ★

Date _____ Place _____

Beer Name _____

Style _____ ABV _____

Brewer _____ Price _____

Appearance—Color, Head, & Clarity _____

_____

Aroma—Hops, Malt, Ethers, & Other Aromatics _____

_____

_____

Taste—Hops, Malt, Balance, & Other Flavors or Factors _____

_____

_____

Mouthfeel—Body, Carbonation, Astringency, Finish, etc. _____

_____

_____

Overall Impressions _____

_____

_____

_____

_____

☐ Draft
☐ Bottle
☐ Can

· · · · · · · · · · · · · ·

RATING

⬜⬜⬜⬜⬜

★ TASTING NOTES ★

Date _____ Place _____

Beer Name _____

Style _____ ABV_____

Brewer _____ Price _____

Appearance—Color, Head, & Clarity _____
_____

Aroma—Hops, Malt, Ethers, & Other Aromatics _____
_____
_____

Taste—Hops, Malt, Balance, & Other Flavors or Factors _____
_____
_____

Mouthfeel—Body, Carbonation, Astringency, Finish, etc. _____
_____

Overall Impressions _____

☐ Draft
☐ Bottle
☐ Can

RATING

⑂ ⑂ ⑂ ⑂ ⑂

★ TASTING NOTES ★

Date _____ Place _____

Beer Name _____

Style _____ ABV _____

Brewer _____ Price _____

Appearance—Color, Head, & Clarity _____
_____

Aroma—Hops, Malt, Ethers, & Other Aromatics _____
_____
_____

Taste—Hops, Malt, Balance, & Other Flavors or Factors _____
_____
_____

Mouthfeel—Body, Carbonation, Astringency, Finish, etc. _____
_____
_____

Overall Impressions _____

☐ Draft
☐ Bottle
☐ Can

RATING

🍺 🍺 🍺 🍺 🍺

★ TASTING NOTES ★

Date _____ Place _____

Beer Name _____

Style _____ ABV_____

Brewer _____ Price _____

Appearance—Color, Head, & Clarity _____
_____

Aroma—Hops, Malt, Ethers, & Other Aromatics _____
_____
_____

Taste—Hops, Malt, Balance, & Other Flavors or Factors _____
_____
_____

Mouthfeel—Body, Carbonation, Astringency, Finish, etc. _____
_____
_____

Overall Impressions _____

☐ Draft
☐ Bottle
☐ Can
· · · · · · · · · ·
RATING

★ TASTING NOTES ★

Date _____ Place _____

Beer Name _____

Style _____ ABV _____

Brewer _____ Price _____

Appearance—Color, Head, & Clarity _____
_____

Aroma—Hops, Malt, Ethers, & Other Aromatics _____
_____
_____

Taste—Hops, Malt, Balance, & Other Flavors or Factors _____
_____
_____

Mouthfeel—Body, Carbonation, Astringency, Finish, etc. _____
_____

Overall Impressions _____

☐ Draft
☐ Bottle
☐ Can

RATING

⬦ ⬦ ⬦ ⬦ ⬦

★ TASTING NOTES ★

Date _____ Place _____

Beer Name _____

Style _____ ABV_____

Brewer _____ Price _____

Appearance—Color, Head, & Clarity _____

_____

Aroma—Hops, Malt, Ethers, & Other Aromatics _____

_____

_____

Taste—Hops, Malt, Balance, & Other Flavors or Factors _____

_____

_____

Mouthfeel—Body, Carbonation, Astringency, Finish, etc. _____

_____

_____

Overall Impressions _____

_____

_____

_____

_____

☐ Draft
☐ Bottle
☐ Can

· · · · · · · · · · · ·

RATING

🍺 🍺 🍺 🍺 🍺

★ TASTING NOTES ★

Date _____ Place _____

Beer Name _____

Style _____ ABV _____

Brewer _____ Price _____

Appearance—Color, Head, & Clarity _____

_____

Aroma—Hops, Malt, Ethers, & Other Aromatics _____

_____

_____

Taste—Hops, Malt, Balance, & Other Flavors or Factors _____

_____

_____

Mouthfeel—Body, Carbonation, Astringency, Finish, etc. _____

_____

Overall Impressions _____

☐ Draft
☐ Bottle
☐ Can

. . . .

RATING

🍺🍺🍺🍺🍺

★ TASTING NOTES ★

Date _____ Place _____

Beer Name _____

Style _____ ABV _____

Brewer _____ Price _____

Appearance—Color, Head, & Clarity _____
_____

Aroma—Hops, Malt, Ethers, & Other Aromatics _____
_____
_____

Taste—Hops, Malt, Balance, & Other Flavors or Factors _____
_____
_____

Mouthfeel—Body, Carbonation, Astringency, Finish, etc. _____
_____

Overall Impressions _____

☐ Draft
☐ Bottle
☐ Can

. . . .

RATING

⛀ ⛀ ⛀ ⛀ ⛀

★ TASTING NOTES ★

Date _____ Place _____

Beer Name _____

Style _____ ABV_____

Brewer _____ Price _____

Appearance—Color, Head, & Clarity _____
_____

Aroma—Hops, Malt, Ethers, & Other Aromatics _____
_____
_____

Taste—Hops, Malt, Balance, & Other Flavors or Factors _____
_____
_____

Mouthfeel—Body, Carbonation, Astringency, Finish, etc. _____
_____

Overall Impressions _____

☐ Draft
☐ Bottle
☐ Can

RATING

🍺 🍺 🍺 🍺 🍺

★ TASTING NOTES ★

Date _____ Place _____

Beer Name _____

Style _____ ABV_____

Brewer _____ Price _____

Appearance—Color, Head, & Clarity _____
_____

Aroma—Hops, Malt, Ethers, & Other Aromatics _____
_____
_____

Taste—Hops, Malt, Balance, & Other Flavors or Factors _____
_____
_____

Mouthfeel—Body, Carbonation, Astringency, Finish, etc. _____
_____

Overall Impressions _____

☐ Draft
☐ Bottle
☐ Can

RATING

⛉ ⛉ ⛉ ⛉ ⛉

★ TASTING NOTES ★

Date _____ Place _____

Beer Name _____

Style _____ ABV _____

Brewer _____ Price _____

Appearance—Color, Head, & Clarity _____
_____

Aroma—Hops, Malt, Ethers, & Other Aromatics _____
_____
_____

Taste—Hops, Malt, Balance, & Other Flavors or Factors _____
_____
_____

Mouthfeel—Body, Carbonation, Astringency, Finish, etc. _____
_____
_____

Overall Impressions _____

☐ Draft
☐ Bottle
☐ Can

. . . .
RATING

⌷ ⌷ ⌷ ⌷ ⌷

★ TASTING NOTES ★

Date _____ Place _____

Beer Name _____

Style _____ ABV_____

Brewer _____ Price _____

Appearance—Color, Head, & Clarity _____
_____

Aroma—Hops, Malt, Ethers, & Other Aromatics _____
_____
_____

Taste—Hops, Malt, Balance, & Other Flavors or Factors _____
_____
_____

Mouthfeel—Body, Carbonation, Astringency, Finish, etc. _____
_____
_____

Overall Impressions _____

☐ Draft
☐ Bottle
☐ Can
. . . .
RATING

🍺 🍺 🍺 🍺 🍺

★ TASTING NOTES ★

Date _____ Place _____

Beer Name _____

Style _____ ABV_____

Brewer _____ Price _____

Appearance—Color, Head, & Clarity _____
_____

Aroma—Hops, Malt, Ethers, & Other Aromatics _____
_____
_____

Taste—Hops, Malt, Balance, & Other Flavors or Factors _____
_____
_____

Mouthfeel—Body, Carbonation, Astringency, Finish, etc. _____
_____
_____

Overall Impressions _____

☐ Draft
☐ Bottle
☐ Can

. . . .

RATING

⊔⊔⊔⊔⊔

★ TASTING NOTES ★

Date _____ Place _____

Beer Name _____

Style _____ ABV _____

Brewer _____ Price _____

Appearance—Color, Head, & Clarity _____
_____

Aroma—Hops, Malt, Ethers, & Other Aromatics _____
_____
_____

Taste—Hops, Malt, Balance, & Other Flavors or Factors _____
_____
_____

Mouthfeel—Body, Carbonation, Astringency, Finish, etc. _____
_____

_____

Overall Impressions _____

☐ Draft
☐ Bottle
☐ Can

RATING

▯ ▯ ▯ ▯ ▯

★ TASTING NOTES ★

Date _____ Place _____

Beer Name _____

Style _____ ABV _____

Brewer _____ Price _____

Appearance—Color, Head, & Clarity _____
_____

Aroma—Hops, Malt, Ethers, & Other Aromatics _____
_____
_____

Taste—Hops, Malt, Balance, & Other Flavors or Factors _____
_____
_____

Mouthfeel—Body, Carbonation, Astringency, Finish, etc. _____
_____
_____

Overall Impressions _____

☐ Draft
☐ Bottle
☐ Can

. . . .

RATING

⑂ ⑂ ⑂ ⑂ ⑂

★ TASTING NOTES ★

Date _____ Place _____

Beer Name _____

Style _____ ABV____

Brewer _____ Price _____

Appearance—Color, Head, & Clarity _____
_____

Aroma—Hops, Malt, Ethers, & Other Aromatics _____
_____
_____

Taste—Hops, Malt, Balance, & Other Flavors or Factors ____
_____
_____

Mouthfeel—Body, Carbonation, Astringency, Finish, etc. ____
_____

_____

Overall Impressions _____

☐ Draft
☐ Bottle
☐ Can

· · · · · · · · · ·

RATING

🍺🍺🍺🍺🍺

★ TASTING NOTES ★

Date _____ Place _____

Beer Name _____

Style _____ ABV _____

Brewer _____ Price _____

Appearance—Color, Head, & Clarity _____
_____

Aroma—Hops, Malt, Ethers, & Other Aromatics _____
_____
_____

Taste—Hops, Malt, Balance, & Other Flavors or Factors ____
_____
_____

Mouthfeel—Body, Carbonation, Astringency, Finish, etc. ____
_____
_____

Overall Impressions _____

☐ Draft
☐ Bottle
☐ Can

. . . .

RATING

⬜⬜⬜⬜⬜

★ TASTING NOTES ★

Date _____ Place _____

Beer Name _____

Style _____ ABV_____

Brewer _____ Price _____

Appearance—Color, Head, & Clarity _____
_____

Aroma—Hops, Malt, Ethers, & Other Aromatics _____
_____
_____

Taste—Hops, Malt, Balance, & Other Flavors or Factors _____
_____
_____

Mouthfeel—Body, Carbonation, Astringency, Finish, etc. _____
_____

Overall Impressions _____

☐ Draft
☐ Bottle
☐ Can

· · · · · · · · · · · · · ·

RATING

🍺 🍺 🍺 🍺 🍺

★ TASTING NOTES ★

Date _____ Place _____

Beer Name _____

Style _____ ABV_____

Brewer _____ Price _____

Appearance—Color, Head, & Clarity _____
_____

Aroma—Hops, Malt, Ethers, & Other Aromatics _____
_____
_____

Taste—Hops, Malt, Balance, & Other Flavors or Factors _____
_____
_____

Mouthfeel—Body, Carbonation, Astringency, Finish, etc. _____
_____
_____

Overall Impressions _____
_____
_____
_____
_____

☐ Draft
☐ Bottle
☐ Can

RATING

🍺🍺🍺🍺🍺

★ TASTING NOTES ★

Date _____ Place _____

Beer Name _____

Style _____ ABV_____

Brewer _____ Price _____

Appearance—Color, Head, & Clarity _____
_____

Aroma—Hops, Malt, Ethers, & Other Aromatics _____
_____
_____

Taste—Hops, Malt, Balance, & Other Flavors or Factors _____
_____
_____

Mouthfeel—Body, Carbonation, Astringency, Finish, etc. _____
_____
_____

Overall Impressions _____

_____

_____

_____

_____

☐ Draft
☐ Bottle
☐ Can
. . . .
RATING

▯▯▯▯▯

★ TASTING NOTES ★

Date _____ Place _____

Beer Name _____

Style _____ ABV_____

Brewer _____ Price _____

Appearance—Color, Head, & Clarity _____
_____

Aroma—Hops, Malt, Ethers, & Other Aromatics _____
_____
_____

Taste—Hops, Malt, Balance, & Other Flavors or Factors _____
_____
_____

Mouthfeel—Body, Carbonation, Astringency, Finish, etc. _____
_____

Overall Impressions _____

- [ ] Draft
- [ ] Bottle
- [ ] Can

....

RATING

🍺🍺🍺🍺🍺

★ TASTING NOTES ★

Date _____ Place _____

Beer Name _____

Style _____ ABV_____

Brewer _____ Price _____

Appearance—Color, Head, & Clarity _____
_____

Aroma—Hops, Malt, Ethers, & Other Aromatics _____
_____
_____

Taste—Hops, Malt, Balance, & Other Flavors or Factors _____
_____
_____

Mouthfeel—Body, Carbonation, Astringency, Finish, etc. _____
_____

Overall Impressions _____

☐ Draft
☐ Bottle
☐ Can

. . . .

RATING

▽ ▽ ▽ ▽ ▽

★ TASTING NOTES ★

Date _____ Place _____

Beer Name _____

Style _____ ABV _____

Brewer _____ Price _____

Appearance—Color, Head, & Clarity _____

_____

Aroma—Hops, Malt, Ethers, & Other Aromatics _____

_____

_____

Taste—Hops, Malt, Balance, & Other Flavors or Factors _____

_____

_____

Mouthfeel—Body, Carbonation, Astringency, Finish, etc. _____

_____

_____

☐ Draft

Overall Impressions _____ ☐ Bottle

_____ ☐ Can

_____ · · · · · · · · · · · ·

_____ **RATING**

_____ ⋃ ⋃ ⋃ ⋃ ⋃

★ TASTING NOTES ★

Date _____ Place _____

Beer Name _____

Style _____ ABV _____

Brewer _____ Price _____

Appearance—Color, Head, & Clarity _____

_____

Aroma—Hops, Malt, Ethers, & Other Aromatics _____

_____

_____

Taste—Hops, Malt, Balance, & Other Flavors or Factors _____

_____

_____

Mouthfeel—Body, Carbonation, Astringency, Finish, etc. _____

_____

Overall Impressions _____

_____

_____

_____

_____

☐ Draft
☐ Bottle
☐ Can

. . . .

RATING

⬇ ⬇ ⬇ ⬇ ⬇

★ TASTING NOTES ★

Date _____ Place _____

Beer Name _____

Style _____ ABV _____

Brewer _____ Price _____

Appearance—Color, Head, & Clarity _____
_____

Aroma—Hops, Malt, Ethers, & Other Aromatics _____
_____
_____

Taste—Hops, Malt, Balance, & Other Flavors or Factors _____
_____
_____

Mouthfeel—Body, Carbonation, Astringency, Finish, etc. _____
_____

_____

Overall Impressions _____

_____

_____

_____

_____

☐ Draft
☐ Bottle
☐ Can

....

RATING

⊔ ⊔ ⊔ ⊔ ⊔

★ TASTING NOTES ★

Date _____ Place _____

Beer Name _____

Style _____ ABV ____

Brewer _____ Price _____

Appearance—Color, Head, & Clarity _____
_____

Aroma—Hops, Malt, Ethers, & Other Aromatics _____
_____
_____

Taste—Hops, Malt, Balance, & Other Flavors or Factors _____
_____
_____

Mouthfeel—Body, Carbonation, Astringency, Finish, etc. _____
_____
_____

Overall Impressions _____

☐ Draft
☐ Bottle
☐ Can

· · · · · · · · · · ·

RATING

🍺 🍺 🍺 🍺 🍺

★ TASTING NOTES ★

Date _____ Place _____

Beer Name _____

Style _____ ABV _____

Brewer _____ Price _____

Appearance—Color, Head, & Clarity _____
_____

Aroma—Hops, Malt, Ethers, & Other Aromatics _____
_____
_____

Taste—Hops, Malt, Balance, & Other Flavors or Factors _____
_____
_____

Mouthfeel—Body, Carbonation, Astringency, Finish, etc. _____
_____

Overall Impressions _____

- ☐ Draft
- ☐ Bottle
- ☐ Can

....

RATING

🍺 🍺 🍺 🍺 🍺

★ TASTING NOTES ★

Date _____ Place _____

Beer Name _____

Style _____ ABV _____

Brewer _____ Price _____

Appearance—Color, Head, & Clarity _____

_____

Aroma—Hops, Malt, Ethers, & Other Aromatics _____

_____

_____

Taste—Hops, Malt, Balance, & Other Flavors or Factors _____

_____

_____

Mouthfeel—Body, Carbonation, Astringency, Finish, etc. _____

_____

_____

Overall Impressions _____

☐ Draft

☐ Bottle

☐ Can

. . . .

RATING

⏄ ⏄ ⏄ ⏄ ⏄

★ TASTING NOTES ★

Date _____ Place _____

Beer Name _____

Style _____ ABV_____

Brewer _____ Price _____

Appearance—Color, Head, & Clarity _____

_____

Aroma—Hops, Malt, Ethers, & Other Aromatics _____

_____

_____

Taste—Hops, Malt, Balance, & Other Flavors or Factors _____

_____

_____

Mouthfeel—Body, Carbonation, Astringency, Finish, etc. _____

_____

_____

☐ Draft

Overall Impressions _____

☐ Bottle

_____

☐ Can

_____

RATING

_____

🍺🍺🍺🍺🍺

_____

★ TASTING NOTES ★

Date _____ Place _____

Beer Name _____

Style _____ ABV_____

Brewer _____ Price _____

Appearance—Color, Head, & Clarity _____
_____

Aroma—Hops, Malt, Ethers, & Other Aromatics _____
_____
_____

Taste—Hops, Malt, Balance, & Other Flavors or Factors _____
_____
_____

Mouthfeel—Body, Carbonation, Astringency, Finish, etc. _____
_____

☐ Draft

Overall Impressions _____

☐ Bottle

☐ Can

. . . .

RATING

◉ ◉ ◉ ◉ ◉

★ TASTING NOTES ★

Date _____ Place _____

Beer Name _____

Style _____ ABV _____

Brewer _____ Price _____

Appearance—Color, Head, & Clarity _____
_____

Aroma—Hops, Malt, Ethers, & Other Aromatics _____
_____
_____

Taste—Hops, Malt, Balance, & Other Flavors or Factors _____
_____
_____

Mouthfeel—Body, Carbonation, Astringency, Finish, etc. _____
_____
_____

Overall Impressions _____

☐ Draft
☐ Bottle
☐ Can

· · · · · · · · · · · ·
RATING

⊔ ⊔ ⊔ ⊔ ⊔

★ TASTING NOTES ★

Date _____ Place _____

Beer Name _____

Style _____ ABV_____

Brewer _____ Price _____

Appearance—Color, Head, & Clarity _____
_____

Aroma—Hops, Malt, Ethers, & Other Aromatics _____
_____
_____

Taste—Hops, Malt, Balance, & Other Flavors or Factors _____
_____
_____

Mouthfeel—Body, Carbonation, Astringency, Finish, etc. _____
_____

Overall Impressions _____

☐ Draft
☐ Bottle
☐ Can

RATING

🍺 🍺 🍺 🍺 🍺

★ TASTING NOTES ★

Date _____ Place _____

Beer Name _____

Style _____ ABV_____

Brewer _____ Price _____

Appearance—Color, Head, & Clarity _____
_____

Aroma—Hops, Malt, Ethers, & Other Aromatics _____
_____
_____

Taste—Hops, Malt, Balance, & Other Flavors or Factors _____
_____
_____

Mouthfeel—Body, Carbonation, Astringency, Finish, etc. _____
_____

Overall Impressions _____

☐ Draft
☐ Bottle
☐ Can

. . . .

RATING

☖ ☖ ☖ ☖ ☖

★ TASTING NOTES ★

Date _____ Place _____

Beer Name _____

Style _____ ABV _____

Brewer _____ Price _____

Appearance—Color, Head, & Clarity _____
_____

Aroma—Hops, Malt, Ethers, & Other Aromatics _____
_____
_____

Taste—Hops, Malt, Balance, & Other Flavors or Factors _____
_____
_____

Mouthfeel—Body, Carbonation, Astringency, Finish, etc. _____
_____

□ Draft
Overall Impressions _____
□ Bottle
□ Can
_____
_____ RATING
_____
_____ 🍺🍺🍺🍺🍺

★ TASTING NOTES ★

Date _____ Place _____

Beer Name _____

Style _____ ABV_____

Brewer _____ Price _____

Appearance—Color, Head, & Clarity _____
_____

Aroma—Hops, Malt, Ethers, & Other Aromatics _____
_____
_____

Taste—Hops, Malt, Balance, & Other Flavors or Factors _____
_____
_____

Mouthfeel—Body, Carbonation, Astringency, Finish, etc. _____
_____

Overall Impressions _____

☐ Draft
☐ Bottle
☐ Can

RATING

⊔ ⊔ ⊔ ⊔ ⊔

★ TASTING NOTES ★

Date _____ Place _____

Beer Name _____

Style _____ ABV _____

Brewer _____ Price _____

Appearance—Color, Head, & Clarity _____
_____

Aroma—Hops, Malt, Ethers, & Other Aromatics _____
_____
_____

Taste—Hops, Malt, Balance, & Other Flavors or Factors _____
_____
_____

Mouthfeel—Body, Carbonation, Astringency, Finish, etc. _____
_____
_____

Overall Impressions _____
_____
_____
_____
_____

☐ Draft
☐ Bottle
☐ Can

. . . .

RATING

🍺🍺🍺🍺🍺

★ TASTING NOTES ★

Date _____ Place _____

Beer Name _____

Style _____ ABV_____

Brewer _____ Price _____

Appearance—Color, Head, & Clarity _____
_____

Aroma—Hops, Malt, Ethers, & Other Aromatics _____
_____
_____

Taste—Hops, Malt, Balance, & Other Flavors or Factors _____
_____
_____

Mouthfeel—Body, Carbonation, Astringency, Finish, etc. _____
_____

_____

Overall Impressions _____

☐ Draft
☐ Bottle
☐ Can

· · · · · · · · · · · ·

RATING

〴 〴 〴 〴 〴

★ TASTING NOTES ★

Date _____ Place _____

Beer Name _____

Style _____ ABV_____

Brewer _____ Price _____

Appearance—Color, Head, & Clarity _____
_____

Aroma—Hops, Malt, Ethers, & Other Aromatics _____
_____
_____

Taste—Hops, Malt, Balance, & Other Flavors or Factors _____
_____
_____

Mouthfeel—Body, Carbonation, Astringency, Finish, etc. _____
_____

Overall Impressions _____
_____

☐ Draft
☐ Bottle
☐ Can
. . . .
RATING

★ TASTING NOTES ★

Date _____ Place _____

Beer Name _____

Style _____ ABV _____

Brewer _____ Price _____

Appearance—Color, Head, & Clarity _____
_____

Aroma—Hops, Malt, Ethers, & Other Aromatics _____
_____
_____

Taste—Hops, Malt, Balance, & Other Flavors or Factors _____
_____
_____

Mouthfeel—Body, Carbonation, Astringency, Finish, etc. _____
_____

☐ Draft
☐ Bottle
☐ Can

Overall Impressions _____
_____

RATING

🍺 🍺 🍺 🍺 🍺

★ TASTING NOTES ★

Date _____ Place _____

Beer Name _____

Style _____ ABV____

Brewer _____ Price _____

Appearance—Color, Head, & Clarity _____
_____

Aroma—Hops, Malt, Ethers, & Other Aromatics _____
_____
_____

Taste—Hops, Malt, Balance, & Other Flavors or Factors ____
_____
_____

Mouthfeel—Body, Carbonation, Astringency, Finish, etc. ____
_____
_____

Overall Impressions _____

☐ Draft
☐ Bottle
☐ Can
. . . .
RATING

⎕ ⎕ ⎕ ⎕ ⎕

★ TASTING NOTES ★

Date _____ Place _____

Beer Name _____

Style _____ ABV _____

Brewer _____ Price _____

Appearance—Color, Head, & Clarity _____
_____

Aroma—Hops, Malt, Ethers, & Other Aromatics _____
_____
_____

Taste—Hops, Malt, Balance, & Other Flavors or Factors _____
_____
_____

Mouthfeel—Body, Carbonation, Astringency, Finish, etc. _____
_____

Overall Impressions _____

☐ Draft
☐ Bottle
☐ Can

. . . .

RATING

▯ ▯ ▯ ▯ ▯

★ TASTING NOTES ★

Date _____ Place _____

Beer Name _____

Style _____ ABV_____

Brewer _____ Price _____

Appearance—Color, Head, & Clarity _____
_____

Aroma—Hops, Malt, Ethers, & Other Aromatics _____
_____
_____

Taste—Hops, Malt, Balance, & Other Flavors or Factors _____
_____
_____

Mouthfeel—Body, Carbonation, Astringency, Finish, etc. _____
_____
_____

Overall Impressions _____

☐ Draft
☐ Bottle
☐ Can

RATING

★ TASTING NOTES ★

Date _____ Place _____

Beer Name _____

Style _____ ABV _____

Brewer _____ Price _____

Appearance—Color, Head, & Clarity _____
_____

Aroma—Hops, Malt, Ethers, & Other Aromatics _____
_____
_____

Taste—Hops, Malt, Balance, & Other Flavors or Factors _____
_____
_____

Mouthfeel—Body, Carbonation, Astringency, Finish, etc. _____
_____
_____

Overall Impressions _____

☐ Draft
☐ Bottle
☐ Can

. . . .

RATING

◻ ◻ ◻ ◻ ◻

★ TASTING NOTES ★

Date _____ Place _____

Beer Name _____

Style _____ ABV_____

Brewer _____ Price _____

Appearance—Color, Head, & Clarity _____
_____

Aroma—Hops, Malt, Ethers, & Other Aromatics _____
_____
_____

Taste—Hops, Malt, Balance, & Other Flavors or Factors _____
_____
_____

Mouthfeel—Body, Carbonation, Astringency, Finish, etc. _____
_____
_____

Overall Impressions _____

_____

_____

_____

_____

_____

- [ ] **Draft**
- [ ] **Bottle**
- [ ] **Can**

. . . .

RATING

★ TASTING NOTES ★

Date _____ Place _____

Beer Name _____

Style _____ ABV_____

Brewer _____ Price _____

Appearance—Color, Head, & Clarity _____
_____

Aroma—Hops, Malt, Ethers, & Other Aromatics _____
_____
_____

Taste—Hops, Malt, Balance, & Other Flavors or Factors _____
_____
_____

Mouthfeel—Body, Carbonation, Astringency, Finish, etc. _____
_____
_____

Overall Impressions _____

☐ Draft
☐ Bottle
☐ Can

· · · · · · · · · ·

RATING

🍺 🍺 🍺 🍺 🍺

★ TASTING NOTES ★

Date _____ Place _____

Beer Name _____

Style _____ ABV_____

Brewer _____ Price _____

Appearance—Color, Head, & Clarity _____

_____

Aroma—Hops, Malt, Ethers, & Other Aromatics _____

_____

_____

Taste—Hops, Malt, Balance, & Other Flavors or Factors _____

_____

_____

Mouthfeel—Body, Carbonation, Astringency, Finish, etc. _____

_____

_____

Overall Impressions _____

_____

_____

_____

_____

☐ Draft
☐ Bottle
☐ Can

· · · · · · · · · · · · · ·

RATING

☖ ☖ ☖ ☖ ☖

★ TASTING NOTES ★

Date _____ Place _____

Beer Name _____

Style _____ ABV _____

Brewer _____ Price _____

Appearance—Color, Head, & Clarity _____
_____

Aroma—Hops, Malt, Ethers, & Other Aromatics _____
_____
_____

Taste—Hops, Malt, Balance, & Other Flavors or Factors _____
_____
_____

Mouthfeel—Body, Carbonation, Astringency, Finish, etc. _____
_____
_____

Overall Impressions _____
_____
_____
_____
_____

☐ Draft
☐ Bottle
☐ Can

. . . .

RATING

🍺 🍺 🍺 🍺 🍺

★ TASTING NOTES ★

Date _____ Place _____

Beer Name _____

Style _____ ABV _____

Brewer _____ Price _____

Appearance—Color, Head, & Clarity _____
_____

Aroma—Hops, Malt, Ethers, & Other Aromatics _____
_____
_____

Taste—Hops, Malt, Balance, & Other Flavors or Factors _____
_____
_____

Mouthfeel—Body, Carbonation, Astringency, Finish, etc. _____
_____

Overall Impressions _____
_____
_____
_____
_____

☐ Draft
☐ Bottle
☐ Can

· · · · · · · · · · · ·

RATING

☐ ☐ ☐ ☐ ☐

★ TASTING NOTES ★

Date _____ Place _____

Beer Name _____

Style _____ ABV _____

Brewer _____ Price _____

Appearance—Color, Head, & Clarity _____
_____

Aroma—Hops, Malt, Ethers, & Other Aromatics _____
_____
_____

Taste—Hops, Malt, Balance, & Other Flavors or Factors _____
_____
_____

Mouthfeel—Body, Carbonation, Astringency, Finish, etc. _____
_____

☐ Draft

Overall Impressions _____ ☐ Bottle

☐ Can

. . . .

RATING

★ TASTING NOTES ★

Date _____ Place _____

Beer Name _____

Style _____ ABV ____

Brewer _____ Price _____

Appearance—Color, Head, & Clarity _____
_____

Aroma—Hops, Malt, Ethers, & Other Aromatics _____
_____
_____

Taste—Hops, Malt, Balance, & Other Flavors or Factors _____
_____
_____

Mouthfeel—Body, Carbonation, Astringency, Finish, etc. _____
_____
_____

Overall Impressions _____

☐ Draft
☐ Bottle
☐ Can

· · · · · · · · · · · ·

RATING

⅂⅂⅂⅂⅂

★ TASTING NOTES ★

Date _____ Place _____

Beer Name _____

Style _____ ABV _____

Brewer _____ Price _____

Appearance—Color, Head, & Clarity _____
_____

Aroma—Hops, Malt, Ethers, & Other Aromatics _____
_____
_____

Taste—Hops, Malt, Balance, & Other Flavors or Factors _____
_____
_____

Mouthfeel—Body, Carbonation, Astringency, Finish, etc. _____
_____
_____

Overall Impressions _____

☐ Draft
☐ Bottle
☐ Can

RATING

〔 〕〔 〕〔 〕〔 〕〔 〕

GLOSSARY

Balance: The degree to which a beer's flavors relate to one another. Desired balance of malt and hops flavors varies by beer style.

Body: The weight of a beer in the mouth, described as light-bodied, medium-bodied, or full-bodied.

Bottom Fermented: Brewed with a type of yeast that sinks to the bottom of liquid during fermentation, which occurs at colder temperatures over a period of weeks or months. Bottom fermenting yeasts create smooth, clear, clean-tasting beers. Lagers are made with bottom fermenting yeasts.

Cask/Bottle Conditioned: Refers to beer that undergoes additional fermentation in bottles or casks with added yeast and, often, sugar. Cask/bottle conditioned beers are unpasteurized, cloudy, and naturally carbonated.

Fermentation: The process by which yeast transforms sugars into alcohol and carbon dioxide.

Finish: The resulting impression of a beer after it has been swallowed.

Hops: Herbaceous flowers that give beer its bitter aromas and flavors. Hops have natural preservative and mild sedative qualities. Many different varieties of hops contribute different aromatic and flavor profiles in beer.

Malt: The most important ingredient in beer, usually made from barley that has been soaked until partial germination, dried or roasted to varying degrees, and ground into grist. Brewers combine different malts to create desired colors, flavors, and aromas.

Pasteurization: The process by which a substance is heated to prevent further microbiological activity. Most people associate the term "pasteurization" with milk, since milk and other dairy products are heat pasteurized in order to stabilize them microbiologically before they hit store shelves. But in the 19th century, Louis Pasteur was busy studying beer, and his pasteurization techniques were applied to beer a whopping 22 years before they were applied to milk.

Reinheitsgebot: The German "beer purity law" that restricts the ingredients in beer to malted barley or wheat, hops, yeast, and water. Many European and American craft brewers still follow this law and advertise their use of traditional ingredients on their beer labels.

Top Fermented: Brewed with a type of yeast that rises to the top of liquid during fermentation, which occurs at warmer temperatures over a period of days. Top fermenting yeasts may impart fruity, spicy, and earthy aromas and flavors. Ales are made with top fermenting yeasts.

Wort: The unfermented liquid produced by "brewing" —or boiling water, malt, and hops—before the yeast is added.

NOTES